Writing History Papers: An Introduction

James D. Bennett

Lowell H. Harrison

FORUM PRESS

Published simultaneously in Canada

Printed in the United States of America

Second Printing, April 1979

Library of Congress Catalog Card Number: 78-66987

ISBN: 0-88273-105-X

Cover Design by Roger Siebe

Contents

Introduction

As a history student, you will almost certainly be required to write papers based upon your research in historical sources. Such research and writing becomes increasingly complex as you progress through the various academic stages; there is a vast difference between what is required in a high school class and what is necessary for the writing of a doctoral dissertation. The higher your academic level, the more likely you are to be involved in writing that will demonstrate your ability to do historical research and to support your findings with footnotes and a bibliography that will demonstrate your mastery of historical techniques.

Unfortunately, your knowledge of research techniques may not be equal to the assignment. You can, of course, acquire a knowledge of research methods through trial and error; the mistakes that lower your grade on a paper should not be repeated again. But this method can be a slow and painful learning experience. We believe that the essential techniques of historical research and writing can be learned more easily and more systematically. This guide is designed to give you practical answers to the most common problems encountered in the writing of history papers.

It is doubtful if any volume could answer all the questions that might arise in doing historical research, and there are many questions that this guide does not attempt to answer. Any guide that tried to be definitive will be so unwieldy as to be unusable for most students. But if you know the fundamentals of research and where to go to find more complicated answers, you will be able to deal with such problems as they arise. Remember that one of your best sources of help for unusual problems is your instructor.

Research styles vary a great deal from one discipline to another and even from one school to another, from one publication to another. No one system is *the* correct one with all others completely wrong. What you must do is (1) adopt a style that is adequate and (2) follow it consistently. In the field of history the recent trend has been toward a simpler style for footnotes and bibliography than was used a few years ago. As you will see later, we have replaced the Latin terms *op. cit.* and *loc. cit.* with a short form of the title, and we have discarded as generally unnecessary such items as the names of publishers and the use of "p." or "pp." before page numbers. In this guide we have followed the styles used by such major historical publications as the *Journal of American History*, the *American Historical Review*, and the *New American*

Nation Series. Our examples, therefore, conform with the tenets of modern historical scholarship.

In writing this guide we have assumed that you are doing a rather extensive term paper or perhaps an honors essay. Thus we progress from a brief discussion of selecting a topic, the necessary first step in writing a paper, to the preparation of a bibliography, the last part of the finished paper. Since this is intended to be a very practical, easily used guide, we have deliberately excluded such important subjects as the nature and philosophy of history and the development of the discipline. Admirable topics for study, their inclusion would have resulted in a quite different and a much longer work.

Researching and writing history can be fun, and we hope that you will enjoy doing it. Don't let yourself be dismayed by research techniques that may be new to you. Master the basic techniques of research and you will be free to concentrate on the more important content of your paper. Technique is essential, but it should never be considered an end in itself.

1
Selecting a Topic

In many instances selecting a topic will be easy for you because your teacher will assign a subject or give you a list of topics from which you will select one. In other cases, however, you may be told to write a paper of some specific length that relates to some aspect of the course. If the choice is yours, these suggestions may be of assistance in helping you make your selection.

1. The subject should be small enough to be handled adequately within the scope of your paper. Don't try to give an account of "The Civil War" or "The Industrial Revolution" in ten pages.

2. But the topic should be important enough to be worth doing.

3. You should be interested in the subject. Work on a topic in which you are interested can sometimes become a chore; work on a topic in which you have no interest can become deadly dull. Try to combine some of your areas of interest and come up with such subjects as "The Camp Music of the Confederate Army" or "Women's Rights in Victorian England."

4. Research materials must be available or obtainable. An otherwise excellent topic may have to be abandoned if your local libraries do not have enough materials for adequate research. On the other hand, you may be able to write on a topic if you can arrange to spend a few days at a larger library that can supplement the materials available to you locally. Copies of specific sources, such as an article, often can be obtained from another library at a reasonable cost, but it is now almost impossible for an undergraduate student to borrow from other libraries on interlibrary loan.

5. You must be competent to handle the materials essential for your research. A topic in Russian history might be impossible for you if much of the material is in Russian and you do not read it. Many topics in political and economic history cannot be done without a good knowledge of statistics.

You are quite likely to start with a topic that is too broad, and as you get into your research you may find that you must narrow the scope of your subject. Chronological and geographical limitations are often the easiest to use, but the best method will vary with your subject. And you may combine two or more approaches. Instead of discussing "The Civil War" superficially in ten pages you might narrow your subject to "The River War in West Tennessee, 1861-1862." Preliminary background reading in your area of interest should help you define a suitable topic from the beginning of your research, but don't hesitate to make changes later if you determine that they are needed. But check with your teacher before making any drastic change.

When you have selected a suitable topic, you are ready to start looking for information on it.

2
Bibliographical Aids

Once a topic has been selected or assigned, you are ready to start collecting material on it. This is an exceedingly important consideration, for inadequate research is not likely to be disguised by the most meticulous use of techniques or fine writing. You must know how to begin finding information on your topic. Once the start has been made, other avenues of research will open up quickly as you examine the footnotes and bibliographies in the sources used. This process resembles the result obtained by tossing a stone into the middle of a small pond. Waves begin to spread out in all directions until they reach the shore, then they turn back upon themselves. When careful research uncovers no new sources, you can be reasonably sure that you have done a comprehensive job.

Exact procedures will, of course, vary from one topic to another and from one library to another. Unless you are very sure of your research abilities, consult with your reference librarians. Knowledge of reference materials is a highly specialized field, and it is a rare historian who cannot benefit from such assistance. But such assistance should be used to supplement your efforts; the librarian is available to help in research, not to do it.

In beginning research there are a few basic starting points which should be examined before starting more detailed searching.

TEXTS

If your paper is being done for a class, or if it falls within the scope of one or more classes, a text or texts will probably be available. Read the pertinent portions to get a general background for your research topic. Pay particular attention to footnotes and bibliography; these afford excellent guides to other sources. Don't trust to memory; make out a list of sources to be examined.

CARD CATALOG

This obvious starting point should be used with more imagination than is often displayed. Read carefully the cards that are listed under your topic and list them for examination. Look for the card or cards that may guide you to related subject headings. For "The Nullification Movement in 1832-33" one would certainly check such subject headings as Andrew Jackson, John C. Calhoun, tariff, states' rights, federalism, South Carolina, and Jacksonian democracy, in addition to nullification. Expect to go back to the catalog as additional topics come to mind.

You should be aware that some libraries do not list their microform (microfilm, microcard, microfiche) holdings in their card catalogs. Check your library's policy on this and, if microforms are not included in the general catalog, be sure to consult the special catalogs and/or lists for this rapidly-growing form of storing information. These catalogs will be found, usually, in the section housing the microform materials. Manuscripts are also often listed in special catalogs.

You may also discover that your library is one that has replaced the card catalog with microfiche cards and readers. Use them as you would a card catalog.

OPEN STACKS

If your library uses open stacks, browse in those sections to which the card catalog has guided you. List the titles that seem promising for more careful examination. Check indexes, using the same imagination to uncover related topics as you did in using the card catalog.

Now you have a growing list of sources (which will continue to grow as you check other footnotes and bibliographies) and a greater familiarity with your subject. You are ready to start using some of the standard bibliographical aids available in most college and many smaller libraries. The reference librarian can help you locate less well-known ones.

GUIDES TO REFERENCE MATERIALS

The wealth of reference materials is almost overwhelming, but, fortunately, there are some guides which supplement the indispensable assistance of the reference librarian.

Frank Freidel, ed., *Harvard Guide to American History* (rev. ed., Cambridge, 1974), 2 vols. Probably the best single source for a researcher in American history. Invaluable discussion of the nature of history, research and writing, the materials of history, research aids, and excellent bibliographies which include articles.

Constance M. Winchell, *Guide to Reference Books* (8th ed., Chicago, 1967), with 3 supplements. A massive guide to reference works in many subject areas.

Jean Key Gates, *Guide to the Use of Books and Libraries* (3rd ed., New York, 1974). Less comprehensive than Winchell but quite useful.

Helen J. Poulton, *The Historian's Handbook: A Descriptive Guide to Reference Works* (Norman, Okla., 1972). An excellent guide that specializes in historical sources.

BIBLIOGRAPHIES OF BIBLIOGRAPHIES

Theodore Besterman, *A World Bibliography of Bibliographies* (4th ed., New York, 1965), 5 vols. International in scope; covers a vast number of subject fields.

The Bibliographic Index (New York, 1938-). Published semi-annually, then combined into more comprehensive volumes. Also international in scope.

Henry P. Beers, *Bibliographies in American History* (New York, 1973). Lists over 11,000 bibliographies on almost every aspect of American history.

DICTIONARIES AND ENCYCLOPEDIAS

Such sources are often very helpful in ascertaining and verifying factual information; many of them indicate sources for additional reading.

Edwin R. A. Seligman and Alvin Johnson, eds., *Encyclopaedia of the Social Sciences* (New York, 1930-35), 15 vols. Many of the articles treat historical topics. Supplemented but not superseded by

Daniel L. Sills, ed., *International Encyclopedia of the Social Sciences* (New York, 1968), 17 vols.

James Truslow Adams, ed., *Dictionary of American History* (rev. ed., New York, 1976), 7 vols. and index. Signed articles on nonbiographical topics, brief bibliographies.

Richard B. Morris, ed., *Encyclopedia of American History* (rev. ed., New York, 1976). Both chronological and topical listings; includes biographical information.

William L. Langer, ed., *An Encyclopedia of World History* (5th ed., rev., Boston, 1972). Sub-title, "Ancient, Medieval, and Modern, Chronologically Arranged." Does not contain bibliography.

BIOGRAPHICAL GUIDES

One does not have to subscribe to the "great man" theory of history to find biographies useful in doing research. For starting points and concise summations, these series are helpful.

Biographical Dictionaries Master Index (Detroit, 1975), 3 vols. A guide to over 725,000 listings in more than 50 works of collective biographies, it tells where to find biographical sketches of a particular person.

Dictionary of National Biography (London, 1885-1921), 22 vols., plus supplements. Biographies of noted dead Britons and British colonists from earliest times to 1950. Useful bibliographies.

Current Biography (New York, 1940-). Useful biographies of contemporary individuals, published monthly, then annually.

Dictionary of American Biography (New York, 1928-44), 20 vols., plus 4 supplements. Signed articles on notable dead Americans. Select bibliography at end of each article.

National Cyclopedia of American Biography (New York, 1892-), 57 vols. to 1977. Contains over 52,000 biographies, including some living persons in current volumes. Use index since subjects are not in alphabetical order.

The Dictionary of American Scholars (New York, 1969), 5 vols., has brief sketches of some 9,500 historians, as well as scholars in other disciplines. A new edition is being prepared.

Who's Who in America (Chicago, 1899-). Biennial dictionary of contemporary American biography. There are many variations of this work, including regional volumes.

There are many more specialized biographical guides in addition to those just listed; reference librarians can help direct you to the appropriate one.

BOOK INFORMATION

Bibliographical information on sources is often incomplete, both for research and for citations. Several guides will help you obtain needed facts.

National Union Catalog to 1942 (Ann Arbor, 1942-46), 167 vols. with subsequent and continuing supplements. Photographic reproduction of Library of Congress printed cards, plus some from other libraries. The various series vary slightly in detail, but generally this is an author and main entry collection. Very helpful in ascertaining bibliographical information.

Book Review Digest (New York, 1905-). Issued ten months each year with annual cumulative volumes. Guide to periodical reviews of current books; good for indicating the value of a source.

Books in Print (New York, 1948-). Annual index to books by publishers listed in *Publishers Trade List Annual;* contains bibliographical information; listed by author, title, and subject.

Cumulative Book Index (New York, 1898-). Ten months a year, then cumulative. World list of books in English language.

GUIDES TO BOOKS IN HISTORY

All of the following references are selective, but they do provide good starting points. Always check the publication date of a source to see how up-to-date it is and how it must be supplemented by more recent sources.

George Matthew Dutcher and others, eds., *Guide to Historical Literature* (New York, 1931). Selective bibliography, under country and subject headings, and index to reviews in professional journals.

George Frederick Howe and others, eds., *Guide to Historical Literature* (New York, 1961). Follows the same general arrangements as Dutcher, ed., *Guide to Historical Literature.*

A Guide to the Study of the United States of America (Washington, D.C., 1960). Bibliography of 6,400 books "reflecting the development of American life and thought."

Grace Griffin and others, eds., *Writings on American History* (1902-). Various compilers and publishers. Excellent annual (but several years have never been done) bibliography of books and articles on American history. Latin America and Canada have been excluded since 1936. A cumulative index covers the 1902-40 volumes. This series will be ended with the publication of the 1961 volume.

A. B. Hart, ed., *The American Nation: A History from Original Sources* (New York, 1904-08), 28 vols. Each volume, done by a specialist in that field, contains a good critical bibliography. Now in preparation, Henry Steele Commager and Richard B. Morris, eds., *The New American Nation Series* (New York, 1954-). This new series will consist of over forty volumes when completed. The bibliographies are excellent.

Cambridge Ancient History (New York, 1923-39), 12 vols., 5 vols. of plates. Fine introduction to the subject with a good bibliography in each volume.

Cambridge Medieval History (New York, 1911-36), 8 vols. Volumes are written by specialists; each contains an excellent bibliography.

Cambridge Modern History (New York, 1902-26), 13 vols., atlas. Very well done with fine bibliographies and detailed index. *A New Cambridge Modern History* (Cambridge, 1957-) is being published. Individual volumes contain no bibliographies and few footnotes, so consult John Roads, ed., *A Bibliography of Modern History* (Cambridge, 1968), which is keyed to the new series.

Cambridge History of the British Empire (New York, 1929-59), 8 vols. Excellent bibliographies in each volume.

GUIDES TO PERIODICALS

In the field of history, a journal is a scholarly publication usually directed to a group of specialists; a periodical is a magazine of a more general nature usually directed to a wider audience. There are scores of historical journals in the United States and many more in other countries. In addition, the historical researcher must remember that journals and periodicals in related fields (geography, economics, political science, agriculture, labor) may contain useful information. Most historical journals are quarterlies which follow much the same format: articles, edited source materials, book reviews, notes of interest to readers. Most of them have an annual index and some have cumulative indexes. Examples of major ones are:

The American Historical Review (1895-). Very comprehensive; any period or area of history in which historians in America might be interested. Now published five times a year.

The Journal of American History (1914-), formerly *The Mississippi Valley Historical Review*. Confines itself to American history.

Journal of Modern History (1929-). Specialized on a chronological basis.

Journal of Negro History (1916-). Specialized by subject but national in scope.

Journal of Southern History (1935-). Specialized on a geographical basis.

Writings in American History and *The Harvard Guide* (both already cited) include references to articles. Among the other guides, these will probably be the most useful:

The Combined Retrospective Index Set to Journals in History, 1838-1974 (Washington & Inverness, 1977-78), 11 vols. *CRIS* is an index by key words to 243 English language periodicals, 1838-1974, including most American historical journals. While not an adequate substitute for the detailed indexes, these volumes are helpful in finding articles devoted in whole or in large part to a particular subject.

Poole's Index to Periodical Literature, 1802-1907 (New York, 1938). This edition includes the supplements issued after first publication. Index to 479 English and American popular periodicals; includes fiction, poetry, and book reviews. Use with *Poole's Index, Date and Key Volume* (Chicago, 1957).

Nineteenth Century Reader's Guide, 1890-1900 (New York, 1944), 2 vols. Index to 51 leading periodicals, chiefly popular ones.

Readers' Guide to Periodical Literature (New York, 1900-). Issued semi-monthly September-June, monthly July-August; cumulative volumes. Indexes articles from over 130 general periodicals including a few historical ones.

Social Sciences and Humanities Index (New York, 1907-). Called *Readers' Guide Supplement* before 1920 and *International Index to Periodicals* from 1920 to 1965; includes more scholarly journals than the *Readers' Guide* and indexes a number of foreign language publications.

Eric H. Boehm, ed., *Historical Abstracts* (Santa Barbara, California, 1955-). A quarterly which abstracts articles from the world's major historical journals and periodicals.

Eric H. Boehm, ed., *America: History and Life* (Santa Barbara, California, 1964-), The five annual publications now include brief abstracts of periodical literature in the field of United States and Canadian history, an index to book reviews, a bibliography that includes books, articles, dissertations, and an annual index.

Eric H. Boehm and Lalit Adolphus, eds., *Historical Periodicals* (Santa Barbara, California, 1961). Annotated list of some 4,500 journals arranged by country and area covered.

Edna Brown Titus, ed., *Union List of Serials in Libraries of the United States and Canada* (3rd ed., New York, 1965). Lists some 156,000 titles in 956 libraries. Very useful for reference work with periodicals. For titles new since 1950 see *New Serial Titles*.

Winifred Gregory, ed., *List of the Serial Publications of Foreign Governments* (New York, 1932). Guide to a type of publication excluded from *Union List of Serials*.

NEWSPAPERS

Newspapers can be quite valuable in historical research, but they must be used with great care for much reporting is hastily done and often inaccurate, and editorial policy may slant even news-stories. Few papers are indexed, so you will do well to postpone newspaper research until you have as much information as possible about specific dates.

N.W. Ayer and Sons Directory of Newspapers and Periodicals (Philadelphia, 1880-). Annual guide; restricted to the United States, Canada, Bermuda, Panama, and the Philippines.

Clarence S. Brigham, *History and Bibliography of American Newspapers, 1690-1820* (Worcester, Mass., 1947), 2 vols. Lists 2,120 papers and gives publishing history and location of files.

Winifred Gregory, ed., *American Newspapers, 1821-1936* (New York, 1937). "A union list of files available in the United States and Canada" in nearly 5,700 depositories.

George A. Schwegmann, Jr., ed., *Newspapers on Microfilm* (Washington, D. C., 1967). Contains about 21,700 entries, a quarter of them foreign, of newspapers found in United States and Canadian libraries.

Herbert Brayer, "Preliminary Guide to Indexed Newspapers in the United States, 1850-1900," *Mississippi Valley Historical Review*, XXXIII (Sept. 1946), 237-58.

New York Times Index (New York, 1913-). Issued semi-monthly, annual cumulative volume. Provides dates for research in other newspapers.

MANUSCRIPTS

On the advanced level, a great deal of historical research is done in manuscript materials; this is less common on the undergraduate level. The location of such collections should be checked for in local and regional historical societies and libraries.

National Union Catalog of Manuscript Collections (Hamden, Conn., 1959-), 14 vols. to date. Lists thousands of manuscript collections in several hundred repositories.

Phillip M. Hamer, ed., *A Guide to Archives and Manuscripts in the United States* (New Haven, Conn., 1961). Lists some 20,000 collections in 1,300 depositories with brief descriptions of major collections.

R. A. Billington, comp., "Guide to American History Manuscript Collections in Libraries of the United States," *Mississippi Valley Historical Review*, XXXVIII (Dec. 1951), 467-96.

MICROFORMS

Most college and university libraries are using various forms of micro-reproductions to expand their holdings, particularly in research materials. Remember that the nature of historical material is determined by what it is, not by the form in which one uses it; microfilming does not change a secondary source into primary material. In addition to items already listed see:

Union List of Microfilms (Ann Arbor, 1951). Lists some 25,000 titles held by 197 institutions through June, 1949. Supplemented by *Union List of Microfilms, 1949-1959* (Ann Arbor, 1961), 2 vols., which has approximately 52,000 titles held by 215 libraries.

Richard Walden Hale, *Guide to Photocopied Historical Materials in the United States and Canada* (Ithaca, New York, 1961). Arranged by geographical area.

GOVERNMENT DOCUMENTS

Government records — federal, state, and local — constitute one of the largest and most valuable bodies of source materials. Almost every library houses some government document titles. High school or local public libraries may have only a few of the most frequently used publications, such as the *Congressional Record* and the annual reports of some of the departments of the executive branch of the federal government (such as the *Yearbook of Agriculture*), but even such limited holdings often can provide a great amount of useful information. Your state library also may be able to make additional documents available through your local library; your librarian can help you in securing this service. College and university libraries, with greater facilities for research, will have larger document collections.

The sheer volume and complexity of government documents make this a difficult field in which to work. Library of Congress classification procedures and those used by other research libraries are not always applicable to government documents. The difficulty of research in government documents should not be used as an excuse to avoid work in this field, however; few historical topics can be dealt with competently without reference to government records. Research and university librarians are aware of the problems documents pose to the beginning researcher and they are generous in the time they will devote to your needs.

You should be aware of the types of material available in document collections and should acquaint yourself with the broad categories used in arranging this material. Publications of the United States constitute by far the largest source of government documents and cover the widest range of categories.

There is no standard method of arranging government documents in a library. Some libraries shelve such material separately, with separate cataloging; some shelve and catalog documents with their other holdings; and some libraries keep government collections separate from their other holdings but list them in their general card catalog with all its other entries. In any case, it is wise to consult the *Monthly Catalog* or the *Documents Catalog* to find particular government documents. If the library in which you are working includes this material in its catalog, items will be difficult to find there unless you know the precise title of the document. Even then, it will be necessary to read a great many cards under the heading "U.S. Government."

The *Monthly Catalog* is used in about the same manner one uses the *Readers' Guide* or some other index to periodicals. Additionally, there are a variety of bibliographies and reference volumes which aid in the location of document material. Laurence F. Schmeckebier and Roy B. Eastin, *Government Publications and Their Use* (2nd rev. ed., Washington, 1969), is such a volume.

Congress

The proceedings of the Congress of the United States constitute one of the most valuable sources of information concerning the activities of the federal government. There are few topics which have not been considered by the United States Congress at one time or another, so the chances are good that the *Congressional Record* will yield at least some information on the topic you are researching. Records of these proceedings are available from the beginning of the government, March 4, 1789, to the present. They have appeared in four series: *Annals of Congress* (1st through 18th Congress, 1st session, March 3, 1789 to May 27, 1824); *Register of Debates* (18th Cong., 2nd sess. to 1st sess. of 25th Cong., December 6, 1824 to October 16, 1837);

Congressional Globe (23rd through 42nd Cong., December 2, 1833 to March 3, 1873); and the *Congressional Record* (43rd Cong., March 4, 1873, to the present).

It should be remembered that there is a new Congress every two years. Prior to ratification of the twentieth amendment to the Constitution, February 6, 1933, the term of a Congress began on March fourth of odd-numbered years; section 2 of the amendment requires that the term shall begin at noon on January third of odd-numbered years, and that the Congress shall meet at least once each year. There also may be additional sessions of Congress, which are designated special sessions of the current number of the Congress.

A volume number is assigned each session of Congress, although each volume is generally printed and bound in many separate parts, the number of parts varying with the mass of material which is to be included. There is an index for each volume of these four series, bound within the volumes in the first three series, but generally appearing as a separate part for the volumes of the *Congressional Record*.

The index to the *Congressional Record* contains both an "Index to Proceedings" and a "History of Bills and Resolutions." The latter is an extremely valuable aid in following the course of legislative action.

Other valuable publications of the Congress are the journal, report, and document series issued by each house. The transcripts of testimony taken before congressional committees holding hearings on bills are generally printed. The decision to print or not to print hearings is made by the committees conducting the hearings. The Congress has never enacted legislation providing for the printing of hearings, and for this reason they are not government publications in the strictest sense. Nevertheless, they have nearly always been used as such. Hearings are known by the name of the Senate or House committee conducting them and are so listed in the *Monthly Catalog*. For this reason it is rather difficult to locate hearings. Unless you are familiar with the range of subjects various committees deal with, it may be necessary to read the entire listing of committees and hearings to find the specific hearing sought.

Courts

The most important materials of the judicial branch of the federal government are the decisions of the Supreme Court, the Courts of Appeals (formerly Circuit Courts of Appeals), and of the District Courts. Decisions of the Supreme Court are printed in *United States Reports*. Prior to 1875 these volumes carried the name of the court reporter who collected them and were referred to by an abbreviated form of the reporter's name. Beginning with volume 91 (1875) they carry their present name, but still in abbreviated form. The citation lists the volume, the abbreviated title and the page, as: 4 *Dal* 175, which indicates volume 4 of the collection made by Dallas, page 175; 91 *U.S.* 205, which is volume 91, page 205, under the name adopted in 1875. The volume numbers are continuous from volume one, 1790, to the present. These volumes contain the Court's (the majority) decision and minority and/or individual opinions when the decision is not unanimous.

Decisions of United States Courts of Appeals and District Courts generally will be of lesser importance to the beginning researcher. Strangely enough, decisions of these courts never have been published in any official manner by the federal government; indeed, no really comprehensive unofficial publication exists covering the years prior to 1880. Nevertheless, for many years decisions of these inferior courts have been published in acceptable form by commercial law printing firms. Decisions of federal Courts of Appeals and District Courts are printed in *Federal Reporter* and *Federal Supplement*, respectively, both published by the West Publishing Company, St. Paul, Minnesota.

Executive Branch

The executive branch of the government accounts for the vast majority of all government publications. In addition to annual reports from most secretaries in the President's Cabinet (the Secretary of State is not required to make an annual report), these executive departments produce a bewildering array of publications dealing with almost every conceivable topic, ranging in form from large bound books (yearbooks of the Department of Agriculture, for example) through pamphlets, brochures, and newsletters. A description or even a listing of these publications is far beyond the scope of this guide; the researcher should seek assistance from a documents librarian.

As a beginning researcher, your needs in this area may be modest: an annual report of the Secretary of the Interior, perhaps, or a specific research bulletin from the Atomic Energy Commission, both of which can be found with little difficulty; or a speech by the President of the United States which, rather surprisingly, may be harder to locate. Despite the great volume and diversity of publications from the executive branch, there is no single source for presidential speeches. Inaugural and state of the union messages, and sometimes other speeches of the President, will be found in the *Congressional Record*, but it may be necessary to check newspapers and compilations (*i.e.*, James D. Richardson, comp., *A Compilation of the Messages and Papers of the Presidents* [New York, c. 1897], 20 vols; Samuel I. Rosenman, comp., *The Public Papers and Addresses of Franklin D. Roosevelt* [New York, 1938-50], 13 vols.) to locate the particular speech you need.

You should know, too, that presidential libraries, containing millions of items relating to the public life of recent presidents (Hoover, Franklin D. Roosevelt, Truman, Eisenhower, Kennedy, Lyndon Johnson) have been established or are in the planning stages. Because of the rapidly increasing volume of such material it seems likely that future presidential papers will not be centrally stored but will be housed in individual presidential libraries.

The basic organization of federal government documents is readily learned, and skill in their use improves with practice. It is obvious, of course, that the greater the researcher's knowledge of the organization and function of government, the easier will be his work with government documents.

State Documents

Publications of state governments generally follow the divisions used in federal government publications. The volume of material published by states is much smaller, of course, and usually is not readily available outside the state's library, which may be located in the capitol building, in a separate building on the capitol grounds, or housed at the headquarters of the state's historical society.

Methods of cataloging and shelving state publications differ from state to state, so that no general directions for locating such material can be given. Professional assistance is absolutely essential to research in this area.

Local Documents

Finally, local governments, agencies, and institutions produce a great amount of document material which may be almost indispensable if you are researching a topic in local history. Records of city council meetings, statistical and other records maintained by such local agencies as city and county health departments, materials collected by local historical societies, and records of churches and parishes, even of private businesses and other institutions, frequently may be helpful. Unfortunately, such material rarely is organized in any systematic manner, and often the material itself may have been stored in any convenient box or closet. Obviously, no instructions can be given to help you in dealing with such situations. The best advice is simply to go to the agency or institution, explain what you are doing and what you are looking for, and ask for help. You may be pleasantly surprised at the lengths to which custodians of local records will go to aid you in your research.

3
Note Taking

Your bibliography of sources to be examined will continue to grow during the process of note taking as you uncover new leads to materials. But somewhere along the line you must start the actual process of taking the notes which will form the basis for your ultimate writing.

You must decide at the outset on certain techniques and use them consistently. Notes should be taken on paper of uniform size to facilitate sorting and filing. Cards are available at college bookstores and stationery counters in three standard sizes: 3" x 5", 4" x 6", and 5" x 8"; some researchers prefer to have regular bond paper cut into appropriate sizes. Such paper is cheaper, but it does not file as well as the stiffer cards. Most card users are likely to select the 4" x 6" intermediate size, but this is a personal matter. The point is to select one size and use no others. Unless you plan to type your notes, the lined cards are most practical.

Typing is, of course, the ideal way of taking notes, but a typewriter can't be used in many libraries where research must be done. Pencil is likely to blur as cards rub together; so you should be prepared with at least two pens to take notes — one always runs out of ink. Some libraries will not permit the use of ink if rare materials are being examined. You need not worry about this; the librarian will inform you of any such restrictions. Unless your script is very legible, print all names, unusual words, or anything else that might be mistaken later.

The first step in taking notes is to make out a bibliography card which contains all of the bibliographical information that you will need for the footnotes and bibliography in your paper. If you are doing extensive research over a considerable period, you should make out a bibliography card even on sources which were consulted but not used. Otherwise, you will find yourself looking into possible sources two or three times as the titles sound promising. In making out the bibliography card, be sure to get the publishing information from the title page, not from the cover or spine of the book or journal. If some publishing information is missing, it can usually be found in the card catalog, the *Union Catalog*, or *Books in Print*. Ideally, your information should be so complete that you never have to go back to the source for additional information.

Some title pages will list several places of publication; unless you know that the company's headquarters are located elsewhere, use the first place named. If a book is one of a series, the full name of the series, the name of the editor, and the volume number in the series should be included on the card. However, if each volume is complete in itself, you may handle it as if it were a single book. You may save yourself time by indicating the call number of the book on the card in case you have to go back to it. If you are doing research at more than one library, even on the same campus or in the same town, indicate beside the call number the library in which the source was found. Many researchers find it helpful in recalling the value of a source to jot a brief comment on the bibliography card; this is especially useful if a critical bibliography is to be written. But remember that the source is judged in terms of its usefulness to you for a particular research project; an excellent work overall could be of little or no value on a particular subject.

Since the bibliography card contains all publishing information that will be required for later use, it is not necessary to duplicate this information on the actual note card. The note card should contain only enough information to guide you to the correct bibliography card without any danger of making a mistake. Some researchers prefer to use numbers; that is, the card shown on page 21 might be "1" and that number placed on any note card immediately indicates its source. Most researchers find it simpler to file bibliography cards in alphabetical order by author. In that case, the heading on a note card might look like this:

Tindall, Emerg. New South

The author's name is not enough, for you do not know that you may not later encounter another work by him. The combination of last name and short title provides an accurate guide to the bibliography card.

This next point is one of the most difficult for beginning researchers to accept: each note card should contain only one topic from one source. The purpose of this dictum is to facilitate filing and arranging the cards and, particularly, the ultimate writing of the paper. If this rule is followed, at the writing stage you should be able to spread out in front of you every bit of information you have relating to a specific point — and there should be no other information on any other subject mixed in with it. This means that you will need to work out a list of topical headings during your preliminary reading before starting your note taking. As you get into your research, you may discover that additional topics need to be added. If you do not rewrite your earlier notes to conform with this one card-one topic rule, you should at least use cross-reference cards to guide you to the cards which contain information on the added topics. If you follow this principle, you may need to start new note cards, each under its own heading, two or three dozen times while taking notes from one very good source. If you have a touch of Scottish blood, you may brood over the unused portion of cards. But the pay-off comes when you get to the writing stage.

Regardless of "waste," never write on the back of a card. This is somewhat expensive but it also facilitates writing, the point at which most historians need all possible assistance. If you follow this suggestion, you waste no time in turning over note cards to see what is on the flip side. All the information you have on a particular topic will be spread before you. If your notes on one topic extend beyond one side of a card, use a paper clip, or a rubber band if there are several cards, to hold them together. Since it is possible for cards to become separated, put enough information on the top of each card to identify the source from which it was taken and the topic it deals with. Add, also, a number for each card after the first. Your heading on the fourth note card might read:

Tindall, Emerg. New South: Negro migration, 4

Example 1: Bibliography Card

author

complete title

complete bibliographical information

Tindall, George B.

The Emergence of the New South

Baton Rouge: Louisiana State University Press, 1967.

Vol. X in Wendell Holmes Stephenson and E. Merton Coulter, eds., A History of the South (Baton Rouge: Louisiana State University Press and The Littlefield Fund for Southern History of the University of Texas, 1947-), 9 vols. to date.

F	WKU	Very useful; good
215	Cravens	critical bibliography
.T59		

call number (this is Library of Congress classification number; many libraries use Dewey classification system)

library where book was found

brief comment on book's value for your research

Example 2: Note Card

author's last name

abbreviated title

topic

card number under this heading

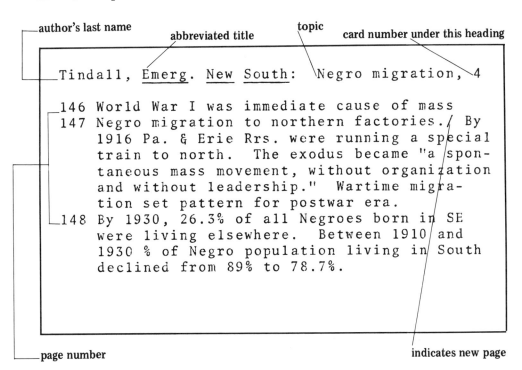

Tindall, Emerg. New South: Negro migration, 4

146 World War I was immediate cause of mass
147 Negro migration to northern factories./ By
    1916 Pa. & Erie Rrs. were running a special
    train to north. The exodus became "a spon-
    taneous mass movement, without organization
    and without leadership." Wartime migra-
    tion set pattern for postwar era.
148 By 1930, 26.3% of all Negroes born in SE
    were living elsewhere. Between 1910 and
    1930 % of Negro population living in South
    declined from 89% to 78.7%.

page number

indicates new page

As you start actual note taking, keep your topic firmly in mind and take only the information that you are reasonably sure you will need. Of course you will sometimes not know at the research stage how extensive your notes should be on a particular topic. In that case, be guided by the availability of the source. If you can easily use it again, restrict your notes and go back later if necessary. But if the source is relatively inaccessible (say in another library), it is better to err by taking too many notes. You may find in some instances when the material being used is both important and lengthy that you save time and money by having it duplicated by Xeroxing or some similar method. But remember that photo-copying of material does not excuse you from studying, analyzing, and absorbing the material; it merely allows you to do so at a more convenient time and with greater accuracy since you will have the material available for frequent reference.

You can minimize note taking if you will paraphrase whenever possible. When we discuss quotations, we'll preach "As few quotations as possible, as brief as possible." The best way to curb the tendency to string together quotations and call it research is to refrain from taking down extensive quotations in the first place. When quotations are used, they must be absolutely accurate, even to the point of including mistakes if there are any. (See page 26 for the use of *sic* to indicate the presence of a mistake.) And be equally certain that you include the exact page or pages from which the quotation is taken. These directions have the further advantage of helping you to avoid plagiarism, which consists of passing off the ideas or work of another as if they were your own. You have committed plagiarism even if you footnote the source, if you let the reader think that the words of the author are yours.

When you get to the footnoting stage, you will have to identify each source by page number. You may indicate the page number in the left-hand margin of your note card; if so, use a slash mark (/) to show the exact point where the pagination changes. Alternately, you can insert the page numbers in the text of your note card, using brackets to fence them off from the contents.

Once you feel that your note taking is substantially complete, the cards must be placed in some kind of order. If you have followed the suggestions given above and have placed headings on your cards, your task is simple. The card headings will constitute a kind of topical outline, and these headings can be juggled around until you come up with an outline which seems logical in its arrangement. Do not feel, however, that once the outline is arranged it must not be changed. After you begin writing you may have a clearer idea about the development of your paper, and changes in the outline may be imperative.

If your notes are extensive, you may find it desirable to arrange cards in some order under the card heading. Such an arrangement may be chronological or topical, or may relate to a specific person or idea; any scheme you choose is fine so long as it aids in the logical development of your paper.

One final warning. Don't feel that you have to use all of your notes when you get to the writing stage. Some notes are made to be destroyed, and you should be ruthless in disposing of them. In all probability, you will compile a mass of notes which will have little or no bearing upon your topic. Don't try to squeeze them in somewhere just because you've got them. Discard the superfluous ones.

4
Writing Your Paper

Writing is an acquired art; few are able to say exactly what they wish to say in the first draft. A readable literary style is the result of laborious writing, correcting, and rewriting. Accept the fact that probably it will be necessary to write and re-write, to tear up and begin again, before you have achieved the best piece of work you are capable of doing. The more writing you do the easier the task will become, and soon you may be writing with greater ease and with more success. The entire process of research and writing will be improved when certain techniques and procedures have become habit. This section will consider those methods and ideas which the writers have found helpful.

Imagination is almost indispensable to the historian. We have already seen that the successful researcher must be a detective in order to ferret out obscure sources and facts; and he must use imagination in the development of his paper. But the historian is bound by the facts of history, unlike the novelist who is free to invent "facts" to permit the development of his story in any way he chooses. This is not necessarily a handicap, however; the historian has in the existing facts a kind of built-in framework which keeps his story within bounds, and truth (that is, fact) is sufficiently varied to give the writer ample leeway to develop his paper imaginatively.

An imaginative approach to and development of a seemingly dull and uninteresting subject often adds significance to a relatively unimportant topic when that topic is placed in its proper setting and tied to the overall picture. The problems of a small textile mill in Massachusetts, fairly insignificant in themselves, may, with proper handling, reveal much about the larger problems of the textile industry in New England and in the nation.

But a word of caution is necessary: do not let your imagination carry you too far afield. Your illustrations and your general treatment of your subject should not be so elaborate and so contrived as to appear artificial. Your major objective, after all, is to communicate some information to someone else. Keep in mind a rather dull reader who has considerably less information on the subject than you have. Will your paper be clear to him? This will lead you to realize that your writing must always be accurate, clear, and consistent.

Clarity is achieved primarily by reading what you have written, keeping in mind the "dull reader" audience, and then revising your manuscript. The importance of rewriting, as a means of achieving clarity and developing a pleasant writing style, cannot be stressed too greatly. Let your manuscript "cool" for a few days before you rework it. When you come back to the work you are likely to see it more objectively than you did when you wrote it. When reworking something you have just written, you are apt to read what you want to say rather than what you actually have said. After allowing the manuscript (and yourself) to cool, you will be better able to see it through the eyes of the "dull reader." A friend who will read your manuscript with a critical eye may also be very helpful to you.

Consistency in your writing is an aid to clarity and an essential factor in developing good style. Lack of consistency is highly annoying to the reader and indicates a lack of discipline in writing. Adopt a set of rules covering the mechanical aspects of writing, such as presented in this manual, and follow those rules. This will add greatly to the smoothness of your style and your work will become easier and faster.

A well-written paper moves smoothly, almost effortlessly, from one idea or concept to the next; the reader is led from one point to the next in a logical sequence. This desirable characteristic is achieved by the use of transitions from one idea to another, and it provides your paper with its essential unity. One sentence should lead logically and effortlessly to the next, a paragraph to the one which follows it. This is achieved by the use (but not the overuse) of key words and phrases, by the use of transitional words such as "however" and "therefore," and by having your material so well-organized that the narrative just flows. In this paragraph we have repeated the key words "logical" and "effortlessly" in order to achieve transition; additional examples are given below:

> It would be impossible to assess the impact of the victory, however, without some knowledge of the country's pre-war condition;

> Although Progressivism is considered a twentieth century development, certain social and economic characteristics of the late nineteenth century provide a setting for the movement;

> Brown's action in this instance was typical of the man, and it reflects the value judgments instilled in him as a child;

> Because one major historian has suggested that Progressivism was a revival of humanitarianism, we should now consider the nation's first great period of reform which occurred in the 1830s and 1840s;

> However, at least three other events should be examined;

> Therefore, several other conclusions are valid.

Do not feel, however, that your research must be absolutely complete, and your notes carefully arranged in final sequence before you begin to write a paper which possesses unity and whose paragraphs flow smoothly from one to the other. You may find that actually writing the paper reveals gaps in what you had thought to be a complete and well-organized outline. Many writers begin the first draft of their manuscript knowing that additional research will be necessary; after reading this preliminary draft they have a clearer idea about what research is still to be done. You can always make additions to these preliminary drafts, and your final copy generally will benefit from the additional revision.

In your writing you will probably make use of primary sources, secondary materials, and your own judgments and conclusions. A primary source is a contemporary, eye-witness account of an event; a secondary source results from the effort of someone who was not present to describe the event. John Quincy Adams' description of a cabinet meeting he attended on November 7, 1823, is a primary source on the background of the Monroe Doctrine; the description of that meeting by a modern diplomatic historian is a secondary account. Historians emphasize primary sources in an effort to discover new material and new insights, but you must not accept as fact each statement from such a source. An account of an event by a dull-witted, unobservant witness would be a primary source, but you could scarcely rely upon its accuracy.

Similarly, you cannot accept uncritically the statements made by even a well-reputed secondary source. Beginning historians are often in awe of the professional historian and particularly of the printed word. You've probably heard someone say, "I know it's true, I read it in the paper." You must not accept without question anyone's statements, no matter how impressive his qualifications and attainments. Even the best of historians make mistakes, and you may have already discovered that equally well-qualified historians may arrive at quite different conclusions after examining the same data. And you cannot rely too much upon your own judgment, because the research that you have done is not likely to have qualified you as an authority on even the limited subject you have been researching.

The good historian tries to ascertain the truth, but he tends to be cautious in his claims. Thus, in most sound historical works you will find frequent qualifications such as "On the basis of available evidence. . . ," or "It seems probable that. . . ." Absolute statements are often the mark of inadequate scholarship.

Historical criticism, the process of evaluating data to determine its usefulness in historical research and writing, is usually divided into two types, external and internal. External criticism consists of learning all that is possible about the source that is being studied, excluding the actual statements contained in it. Who was the author? Under what circumstances did he write? Was he a biased observer? Is the source original or a copy? If the latter, is it an accurate copy? Has it been edited? Such an examination of a source can become very complicated and require the talents of an expert in the field. In other instances, the necessary question or questions may be easily answered.

When James Truslow Adams wrote *The Adams Family*, he knew that a careful reader would wonder if it was another adulatory family history. So the first sentence in his preface contained this disclaimer: "The family whose story is told in this volume (and with which I am in no way connected) is the most distinguished in the United States." Much more complicated was the history of a map. In 1965 after several years of close examination, Yale University scholars announced the discovery of a map dating from about A.D. 1440 that depicted the Greenland coast in accurate detail, and thus proved conclusively that Europeans were acquainted with America well before 1492. One disturbed Columbus advocate called the discovery "a Communist plot," but historians saw it as "the most exciting cartographic discovery of the century." Then, in 1974, a Yale spokesman ruefully announced that sophisticated chemical tests had shown that the ink used on the map had not existed prior to the 1920s. The Vineyard map was a very skillful modern forgery.

Internal criticism involves an examination of the statements contained in the source. Are they true or false? Or, what is more common and more confusing, are they partially true and partially false? A statement is what someone has said about something; it may or may not be a fact. Before an historian can use a statement, he must try to ascertain its truthfulness. As a careful historian, you should be skeptical of any statement until you have examined it critically — and you should retain some doubts even then. Suppose you encounter this statement that Thomas Jefferson wrote in 1787: "The tree of liberty must be refreshed from time to time with the blood of patriots and tyrants. It is its natural manure." Does this statement mean what it seems to say? Did Jefferson mean that bloody revolutions at frequent intervals were essential to a free government? Is such a view consistent with your knowledge of Jefferson and his career? Could he be exaggerating to make a point? Did he ever refer to his election as "the Revolution of 1800?" Could he have meant something like rotation in office rather than a revolutionary bloodbath? Can you accept and use his statement at face value?

As you examine historical materials, ask yourself the questions that a shrewd lawyer might ask a hostile witness on cross-examination. And even after you have formulated your conclusions, remain willing to subject them to further scrutiny as more evidence becomes available and as you ponder over the evidence you have. Historical criticism is one of the most difficult tasks confronting the historian; it is also one of the most important.

See pages 59-60 for citations to some problems in historical criticism that historians have tried to solve.

The information presented thus far should prepare you rather well for completing the final draft of your paper; some comments on grammar and general use of language may provide additional help, however. These comments are certainly not original with us and, as a matter of fact, they will be found in any good book on grammar and usage; if you are a good student of the English language, most of them will be familiar to you. They are given here primarily for convenience.

SOME DO'S AND DON'TS FOR WRITING

Your paper should be written in the past tense and in the active voice.

Do not make changes in quoted material in order to correct either grammar or fact. Suppose that this is your quotation: "It don't make any difference to me." You are not at liberty to correct the grammar, but you certainly do not want to be credited with the error. This, and similar errors, are handled by using the Latin "*sic*," meaning "thus," placed in brackets immediately following the error:

It don't [sic] make any difference to me.

This form indicates that the quotation is accurate, even in its error, and that you are aware of the fault.

If a mistake is not so obvious, you can help your reader by showing the correction in brackets in place of *sic* :

The charge was led by D. H. Hill [A. P. Hill] who arrived just in time.

Brackets also are used to enclose an author's comments. They should, however, be used sparingly. Extensive comments will probably be more appropriate in a footnote.

You should avoid using contractions (use "did not" rather than "didn't"), and trite phrases ("as luck would have it").

Slang and "cute" expressions have no place in your research paper.

Avoid both choppy sentences and highly complex sentences — neither will help you achieve your goal of clear, smooth-flowing paragraphs.

Be concise. Make your statement clearly, and make it only once.

Avoid indefinite pronouns; pronouns must be used to avoid endless repetition and to add variety to your style, but you must be sure that the noun to which the pronoun makes reference is perfectly clear.

Avoid personal pronouns which refer to the author and the reader, such as "I," "me," and "we." Certain other pronouns ("her," "she") will be used a great deal, of course. The statement, "I want to say that Brown did everything well," does not belong in a research paper.

Do have agreement in number:

"He gave each man his books," not "He gave each man their books."

Avoid redundancy:

Say "continue" rather than "continue on;" "refer" rather than "refer back."

Use parallel construction. Avoid a statement such as this:

"He admired the painting because its composition was pleasing and for the way it makes you feel."

Avoid abbreviations in the body of your paper. U.S. Cong., while perfectly acceptable in a footnote, should not be used in the body of the paper.

Do not use titles such as Doctor, Professor, Mister, General, or Justice in footnotes or bibliography; use them sparingly in the text.

Numbers from one through nine in the text of your paper should be spelled; others should be written in Arabic numerals, with this exception: if the number begins a sentence, it should be spelled.

Be sure you know the meaning of the words you use.

Make a carbon or a photo copy of your paper, and correct it just as you correct the ribbon copy. This is insurance against the possibility that the ribbon copy may be lost.

Do not capitalize the word after a colon unless it is a proper name.

5

Mechanics of Term Papers

Typewritten papers are more readable than those written in longhand, and they make a much better appearance. Because most students are able to type and have access to typewriters, or can secure the services of a typist for a nominal charge, there is little reason to submit a handwritten paper.

After you have completed research and have written and corrected preliminary drafts of your paper, there remains the hurdle of typing the final draft. This chore becomes less difficult if you have your first draft in proper shape before you begin typing; then it involves adhering to certain rules which constitute the mechanics of paper writing. Many schools have simplified this procedure by preparing manuals of style which must be followed for papers submitted to them. If such a manual is not available, the material in this section should give you sufficient information to complete the job satisfactorily.

Division headings should not be used in short papers. Unless a paper is sufficiently long to be divided into chapters containing at least 15 to 20 pages each, there is no need for headings. Most term papers, therefore, will not be long enough to warrant division headings. Obviously, a thesis or an honors essay will be much more complicated and considerably longer. Many departments or schools will have specific guides for longer works.

Whether you do your own typing or have it done, you alone are responsible for the accuracy and appearance of the final draft. A typist will give due regard to the appearance of the paper and will produce a faithful copy of the manuscript you have given him or her. All changes and corrections should be clear and easily understood, footnotes and bibliography should be in proper form, both pages and footnotes should be correctly numbered and in order, and the footnotes should be on the proper pages. This calls for careful proofreading before final typing and again after the typescript is completed.

Inevitably there will be some errors; if these involve more than the correcting of one or two letters, it is probably best to retype the entire page. With such conveniences as "Corrasable Bond" and "Correctape," however, it is possible to erase an entire word and replace it with the correct word, but this requires a good deal of skill. Care must be taken to type in the correct word with the same touch on the keys which was used for the original word, else the correction will detract from the appearance of the page. If the error is not noticed at the time it is made, the difference in length of the incorrect and correct words may make it impossible to make the correction. In retyping a page the last line of the new page must be properly filled out with neither unused space nor excess words. It is easier to make corrections before the page is removed from the typewriter; however, if the error is found after the page is removed, it is better to correct the original and all copies separately rather than to re-stack the pages and carbons.

Any correction which would be noticeable should not be attempted; rather, the page should be retyped. Your object is to prepare a neat, accurate paper which is easy to read and pleasing to look at.

TYPING FOOTNOTES

Notes are so important that they should be placed at the bottom of the appropriate page for convenient reference by the interested reader (hence the term, "footnotes") rather than at the end of the paper ("endnotes"). This procedure is not so difficult as it may seem; an easily-made guide will enable you to place the footnotes correctly at the bottom of the appropriate pages.

This guide sheet should be the same length as your typing paper, and one-half inch wider. On the half-inch extension of the guide sheet mark the top and bottom typing margins. Then, beginning at the bottom margin and going upward, number (using the typewriter) each line, with the last (and largest) number at the top margin. Next, stack your paper for insertion in the typewriter in this order: the guide sheet, second sheet, carbon (dull side up), and typing page. Keep left, top, and bottom margins aligned and place in typewriter. When this is done, the guide sheet will extend to the right of your typing paper and the line numbers you have typed on the guide sheet will be visible. You will know how many lines you have remaining after each line is typed. When you have typed approximately half a page, count the number of footnote numbers you already have put on the page and add to that the number of footnote numbers in the next half-dozen lines of manuscript. Count the number of lines which will be required for each note, add double-spacing between each note, the double-spaces before and following the solid line which separates text and notes, and the line for the solid line itself, and subtract the total from the number remaining on the guide sheet. This will give you the number of the last line of type on the page, and will give you precisely the number of lines necessary for placing your notes at the bottom of the page. While this procedure may sound complicated, it is easier done than explained. A little practice will make you proficient at placing footnotes on the page.

TYPEWRITER

When your paper is ready to be typed, you (or your typist) must see to it that your machine is in proper condition before beginning your paper.

Two styles of typeface, elite and pica, usually are available on standard typewriters. Either is generally accepted, but the larger pica type is preferable. Electric typewriters offer greater variety in type choices and most are acceptable. Script, italic, or similar type styles are not acceptable for a paper.

The machine should be thoroughly cleaned before you begin typing your paper. Special brushes and cleaning liquids are available for cleaning the roller (platen) and the typefaces.

Make sure that your ribbon is either new or in very good condition, and that you have sufficient ribbons of the same type to complete the work. The ribbon color

Example 3: Last Page of Paper or Chapter

it is that Turner's "abiding faith in democracy" gleams in this unfinished last work of one of America's outstanding historians. We may not agree with a reviewer that "had it been finished it undoubtedly would have been [his] masterpiece," but we would find it difficult to take issue with the statement that the book "makes for the completeness" of Turner's career.[80]

---

[80]Lamar, "Frederick Jackson Turner," 99; Roy M. Robbins, "Review of The United States 1830-1850; The Nation and Its Sections," Mississippi Valley Historical Review, XXII (Sept. 1935), 295-97.

should be black, and it should not be used to the point where the characters appear dim on the page. You may find it wise to rotate several ribbons, at regular intervals, if you are typing a long paper. The use of a carbon ribbon, available for most typewriters, solves this problem nicely.

PAPER

Many schools and/or departments have established quality standards for acceptable typing paper. If your school or department has not, you will be safe in using white 20 pound weight, 50 percent rag content bond for your original, or ribbon, copy. A lighter weight paper (often called "onion skin") is generally acceptable and often desirable for copies, but photo copying is often used instead of carbons, especially if several copies are needed.

Carbon paper should be black, hard-finish, non-smearing, and of a medium or light weight.

Always keep a carbon or photo copy of your paper.

MARGINS

A one-inch margin should be left on all sides of the paper, with these exceptions:

1. Leave a two-inch margin at the top of the first page of each major division of the paper.

2. If you plan to bind your paper, use a left margin of either one-and-one-half or two inches.

SPACING AND INDENTATION

The text of the paper should be double-spaced. Footnotes and bibliographical entries are typed single space and separated from each other by double spaces. Paragraph indentation may be from five to eight spaces, and must be consistent. Quotations of more than two sentences, or quotations which consume more than four lines of type, should be single-spaced and separated from the double-spaced text by two spaces before and two spaces following the quotation. Traditionally, the "extended quotation" is also indented on both sides, but the current trend in historical journals is toward the elimination of indentation. Some journals are following a middle-of-the-road policy by indenting the left margin of the quotation and keeping the right margin flush with the text margin. Again, no one style is correct; select one form and adhere to it. If you choose to indent either the left or both margins, the indentation may be the same space set for paragraph indentation. When the quotation includes the first line of a paragraph, it is additionally indented, the same number of spaces as paragraphs in the text. Quotation marks are not used with indented quotations, for the special form indicates that it is a quotation. Additional information concerning the indentation of footnote and bibliographical material will be found under those headings.

PAGINATION

Each page of the paper, except the blank page which follows the title page, has a number, although the number is not shown on the title page. Preliminary parts of the paper, which precede the actual text, are numbered in small Roman numerals centered at the bottom of the page and three-fourths of an inch from the edge of the paper. Thus, the first number to appear would be "ii." The text of the paper is numbered in

Arabic numerals which, with the exception of the first page of chapters, should be located in the upper right-hand corner of the page. The beginning page of each chapter is numbered at the bottom of the page, in the same place as the numbers for the preliminary pages. The first page of the first chapter (or the first page of text of your paper) is numbered "1" and the numbering continues consecutively throughout the remainder of the paper, including text, illustrations, appendices, and bibliography.

UNDERLINING

Underlining is used to indicate the title of published works, to identify foreign phrases, and to add emphasis to certain words or phrases in your paper. You will be concerned primarily with the underlining of titles.

Underline the title of all complete, published works — books, journals, magazines, newspapers, and similar publications — and place within quotation marks the titles of parts of them — such as the title of a chapter in a book or the title of an article in a learned journal, as well as unpublished materials — typed reports, minutes, theses, and similar written but unpublished material. Underline the entire title of the publication wherever it appears in your paper and, in footnotes, the capital letter abbreviations for well-known publications (MVHR, AHR) that are being used extensively. We prefer the practice of underlining words only, and have followed that practice in this manual, but it is permissible to underline the spaces between words as well as words, by use of a continuous line from the first through the last letter of the title. Compare the examples here, make your choice, and follow it consistently:

> John C. Brown, The Writing of the Constitution
> John C. Brown, The Writing of the Constitution

PARTS OF THE PAPER

There are three main parts of a paper: preliminaries, text (or body), and reference material. (Few papers will contain all of the parts mentioned here, but the parts of your paper should be arranged in this order, regardless of omissions.) The preliminaries consist of the title, preface, acknowledgments, table of contents, lists of tables and illustrations. The reference material contains appendices and bibliography. Major divisions within a paper are begun on a new page and are given a heading. The heading should be centered on the page, two inches from the top. If the length of the heading would cause it to begin to the left of the paragraph indentation, two or more lines should be used, in inverted pyramid fashion, and with two spaces between each line. (The second line should be typed on the third space below the first line of the heading.) The entire heading is typed in capitals and no terminal punctuation is used.

Title Page

Your teacher will probably indicate the desired form for the title page, or the form will be prescribed by the department or school. If not, the following information should appear on the title page: complete title, in capitals, without quotations, and with internal punctuation only (commas, semi-colons, colons). The title should be centered on the page, at least two inches from the top. If the title is lengthy, more than one line should be used, each line being separated by double spaces. Additional information (student's name, course name and number, date) should be centered on the page in the lower half of the paper. This material is capitalized in the ordinary manner, *i.e.*, it is not typed entirely in capitals. All information placed on the title page should be suitably arranged and balanced to produce a pleasing, uncluttered appearance. See pages 35-36 for examples of a title page.

Preface

This section usually is omitted in a short paper. When it is used, it is not an introduction to the study but a comment on the reasons for making the study, and/or its scope or purpose. The preface may also contain acknowledgment of help which you received from individuals and from libraries or other institutions. If you have no comment to make concerning the paper, this section should be titled "Acknowledgments" rather than "Preface." Other sections of the prefatory material are self-explanatory.

Reference Material

The bibliography and one or more appendices are included in this section. An appendix is not required, but you may use it to present substantive material which is not considered sufficiently important to include in the text but which the reader would find helpful to consult, and which may not be readily available elsewhere. But resist the impulse to include material in an appendix just because you have some notes that you could not use in the text. The bibliography lists the sources, both primary and secondary, which you have used in writing your paper. It is sometimes necessary to divide the bibliography into several divisions, which will be discussed in another section.

Example 4: Title Page

A NEW DEAL FOR MUSCLE SHOALS: CREATION

OF THE TENNESSEE VALLEY AUTHORITY

Carol Crocker
History 348
May 21, 1978

HENRY WIRZ:

THE LAST VICTIM OF ANDERSONVILLE

An Honors Essay
Presented to
the Faculty of the Department of History
Western Kentucky University
Bowling Green, Kentucky

In Partial Fulfillment
of the Requirements for the
History Honors Program

by
Denise Ruth Walker
May 1978

6
Footnotes

Footnotes are an indispensable part of historical scholarship and a distinguishing characteristic of scholarly work, although their presence does not guarantee a scholarly manuscript.

Footnotes serve two major purposes for historians. First, they indicate the exact source or sources from which material was obtained. A critical reader will not accept your opinion or version of events without knowing the evidence upon which it is based. As you do historical writing, you might think of yourself as a lawyer presenting a case in court. Your footnotes are the witnesses which, you hope, will convince a skeptical jury that your case is sound and your conclusions valid. A lawyer may call several witnesses to stress a particularly critical point; this is one of the main reasons for multi-citation footnotes. Both the lawyer and the historian will try to present the best obtainable testimony; prejudiced, biased, inaccurate accounts are likely to do more harm than good.

Secondly, "content footnotes" are used to add pertinent information to what is included in the text. While this is often desirable and sometimes necessary, it presents a dangerous temptation which you must learn to resist. Far too often, a researcher uses footnotes as a repository for information which did not fit into the text but which he just could not bear to discard. You must remember that many of your notes should be discarded at the writing stage; resist the impulse to enshrine them in footnotes just because you went to the trouble of taking down the information. If a content footnote is very long, it may be important enough to be included in the text — or so irrelevant as to demand abandonment.

The footnote is indicated in the text, after the material to which it refers, by an Arabic number raised above the line for easy visibility; there is no period after the number. Notes are numbered consecutively throughout the entire paper or chapter. The footnote number should come at the end of a sentence. If it must appear within a sentence, try to place it at a punctuation break. The use of multi-citation footnotes usually will render unnecessary notes within a sentence, and will help avoid an excessive number of footnotes.

Footnotes are separated from the text by a solid line of fifteen spaces typed from the left-hand margin. Notes are indented the same number of spaces as a paragraph in the text (usually five), and each note is considered as a paragraph. Footnotes are usually indicated by an unpunctuated Arabic number raised above the line with no space between the number and the first word in the note. But the footnote number is easily visible because it is the first thing in a note, and some instructors permit the number to be typed on the line, a concession which facilitates typing. If this is done, a period follows the number. Only one note should appear on a line, no matter how much space is left over, and every effort should be made to avoid running a note onto another page. If this must be done, do not repeat the number of the note on the second page. Footnotes are single-spaced to indicate the smaller type in which they are usually printed. Double-space, however, between notes.

A single footnote may, of course, include citation to one or more sources and content material. See example 35 below.

Historians are confronted with the chronic problem of when to use a footnote. Unfortunately, absolute rules just do not exist; the harassed author (with the aid of a few general guidelines) must play it by ear.

Do not footnote information which is assumed to be common knowledge; you can write "After Columbus reached America in 1492 . . ." without documenting that fact. But what is common knowledge for one reader may not be for another. As a novice, you should err by having too many notes rather than too few. As you acquire more confidence in writing, your use of footnotes will probably decrease.

But the reader has the right to know where you found any exact quotation cited and what your authority was for any statement which might attract dissent.

Notes are subordinate to the text, and you must keep them in that status. Excessive devotion to footnotes usually results in choppy, fragmented writing.

Anyone who does much historical writing knows that footnotes can become very complex and tricky. Some sources almost defy efforts to follow a regular form, and it would be futile to attempt to supply examples of all the exotic types. But the great majority of footnotes you will use can be indicated in a few dozen examples. As for the rest, improvise from standard forms and ask your instructor. Once you have an acceptable form, follow it exactly thereafter.

Inexperienced historians sometimes become frustrated with the admonition to follow exact forms without deviation and complain that it really makes no difference if a comma is always at the same spot. Our insistence upon exactness does not stem from either a pedantic devotion to detail or a sadistic desire to inflict intellectual pain. When you have mastered the techniques of a good research system, you can then focus your attention upon the writing of your paper. Yet you will know, without having to think about them, that the proper techniques are being followed. Mastery of detail will not enslave you; on the contrary, it will free you for more important work.

The following examples will provide models for most of the footnotes that you will use. Notice that in this modern style no publisher is given and no "p." or "pp." is used before the page numbers. Get the publishing information from the title page of the publication, never from the spine or a binding which has been added. If more than one place of publication is given in a book, use the one on the left. The numbers below are example numbers, not footnote numbers as they would appear in a paper.

BOOKS

Standard form

```
    1.  Moorfield Storey, Charles Sumner (Boston,
1900), 431.
```

Obscure place of publication

```
    2.  Loren Baritz, The Servants of Power (Middle-
ton, Conn., 1960), 37.
```

Multi-editors, multi-volumed, published over several years

     3.   Edward Waldo Emerson and Waldo Emerson Forbes, eds., The Journals of Ralph Waldo Emerson (10 vols., Boston, 1909-1914), X, 294.

Volume in a series

     4.   Thomas P. Abernethy, The South in the New Nation (Baton Rouge, 1961), in Wendell Holmes Stephenson and E. Merton Coulter, eds., A History of the South (9 vols. to date, Baton Rouge, 1948-), IV, 37.

If a volume is complete in itself it is sometimes cited without reference to the series of which it is a part.

Later edition

     5.   Arthur S. Link, American Epoch: A History of the United States Since the 1890's (2nd ed., rev., New York, 1963), 221.

Sponsoring organization instead of author

     6.   Department of the Army, The United States in the World War, 1917-1919 (17 vols., Washington, 1948), X, 22.

Date of first publication deemed necessary. Not usually required; see example 5.

     7.   George E. Mowry, The California Progressives (Chicago, 1963; first published 1955), 73.

Section of longer work

     8.   Frederick M. Davenport, "Did Hughes Snub Johnson? An Inside Story," David Farrelly and Ivan Hinderacker, eds., The Politics of California (New York, 1951), 208-11.

ARTICLES

Cite specific page numbers, not the entire article. For volume number, use Arabic or Roman numerals, depending upon what is on the cover or title page of the issue, not what is on the spine of the bound issue. Notice that no use is made of the issue number which often follows volume number.

Historical journal

     9.   Christopher Lasch, "The Anti-Imperialists, the Philippines, and the Inequality of Man," Journal of Southern History, XXIV (Aug. 1958), 319.

Magazine, signed article

     10.   Walter V. Bingham and James Rorty, "How the Army Sorts Its Manpower," Harper's Magazine, 185 (Sept. 1942), 436.

Magazine, unsigned, untitled

11.   <u>Newsweek</u>, LXVIII (Aug. 22, 1966), 25.

Magazine, titled but unsigned

12.   "Sex O'clock in America," <u>Current Opinion</u>, LV (Aug. 1913), 113-14.

PROCEEDINGS

13.   Gilbert Chinard, "The American Philosophical Society and the World of Science, 1768-1800," <u>Proceedings of the American Philosophical Society</u>, LXXXVII (1943), 5.

NEWSPAPERS

The name of the city is not underlined unless it is part of the title, but the place of publication is always given. If the city is not well known or could be confused with another, indicate the state or country in which it is located. Notice in example 17 that an author and title may be used. Page numbers are normally not cited, although they may be for something like an article in the New York *Times* Sunday magazine section.

14.   New York <u>Gaelic American</u>, Dec. 21, 1918.

15.   Springfield (Mass.) <u>Republican</u>, Feb. 12, 1903.

16.   <u>Courier and New York Enquirer</u>, Dec. 19, 1856.

17.   Dorothy Dix, "A Modern Diana," <u>Boston American</u>, April 7, 1910.

18.   <u>Boston American</u>, July 14, 21, 1916; New York <u>Times</u>, Feb. 6, 1917.

MANUSCRIPTS

Both the name of the collection and its location must be given in the first citation. As example 21 indicates, subsequent citations do not repeat the location, and the title of the collection may be shortened.

19.   House Diary, Nov. 12, 1913, Edward M. House Papers (Yale University Library).

20.   Walter Hines Page to William Jennings Bryan, March 17, 1914, William Jennings Bryan Papers (Manuscript Division, Library of Congress).

21.   House Diary, Nov. 13, 1913, House Papers.

22.   Fees Paid to Benoni S. Garland, Dec. 13, 1859, Estate of John F. A. Sanford, No. 5328 (1858-1862), Probate Court, St. Louis (Clerk's Office).

23. Henry L. Dawes, "Gen. Butler and Richard H. Dana," manuscript article in Henry L. Dawes Papers (Manuscript Division, Library of Congress).

24. Eric Geddes to David Lloyd George, Private and Personal, Oct. 13, 1918, Drawer 90, Folder 53, William Wiseman Papers (Yale University Library).

In example 25 the author felt it necessary to identify the location of the author of the letter. "Author" here means the author of the paper, and the form implies that the letter is still in his possession.

25. John S. Goff, Phoenix, Arizona, to author, April 19, 1969.

GOVERNMENT DOCUMENTS

The title in example 32 is so lengthy that it needs to be shortened drastically for subsequent citation. The reader could not be expected to recognize the short form (OR), so this must be indicated in the first citation to the source.

26. Cong. Record, 62 Cong. 2 Sess., 2815-33 (March 5, 1912).

27. U.S. Statutes at Large, XXXVII (Washington, 1913), Part I, 560-69.

28. Senate Doc., 66 Cong., 1 Sess., No. 106 (Serial 7605), 795-98.

29. Plessy v. Ferguson, 163 U.S. 537 (1896).

30. Department of Interior, Office of the Census, Eleventh Census of the United States: 1890. Population (25 vols., Washington, 1895), Vol. I, pt. 1, p. 471.

31. Department of State Bulletin, I (Sept. 23, 1939), 277.

32. The War of the Rebellion: A Compilation of the Official Records of the Union and Confederate Armies (128 vols., Washington, 1880-1901), Ser. I, Vol. XXXVIII, Pt. III, 678-80. Hereafter cited as OR.

THESIS, DISSERTATION

The absence of an underlined title shows that this thesis was used in an unpublished form.

33. Richard M. Dalfiume, "Desegregation of the United States Armed Forces, 1939-1953" (doctoral dissertation, University of Missouri, 1966), 30-57.

CONTENT NOTE

This example shows a citation and content note.

34.   Washington (Ky.) Mirror, Nov. 17, 1798.
There are several discrepancies in the accounts given
in the Journal and the newspapers, especially as to
dates. Since the Journal gives no account of debates
in the committee of the whole, the newspaper accounts
have been helpful in tracing the progress of the Resolutions.

MULTI-CITATION

35.   Thomas Ashe, Travels in America in 1806
(New York, 1811), 38; Gilbert Imlay, A Description of
the Western Territory of North America (Dublin, 1793),
33-34; Bayrd Still, "The Westward Migration of a Plant-
er Pioneer in 1796," William and Mary Quarterly, 2nd
Series, XXI (Oct. 1941), 327. See also Everett Dick,
The Dixie Frontier (New York, 1948), 19.

INTERVIEWS

The first interview was conducted by the author of the paper, the second by
someone else.

36.   Interview with Gardner Smith, July 17, 1967.

37.   Interview, Gardner Smith by James F. Howard,
May 13, 1969, James F. Howard Collection (Kentucky
Library, Western Kentucky University).

If the interview has been taped use this form:

Interview, Gardner Smith by James F. Howard, May
13, 1969. Tape on deposit in the Oral History Archives (Western Kentucky University).

MISCELLANEOUS

Review

38.   E. Bradford Burns, review of Robert Brent
Toplin, The Abolition of Slavery in Brazil (New York,
1972), in Civil War History, 19 (June 1973), 179-180.

Lecture

39.   M. B. Lucas, class lecture, History 401B,
Western Kentucky University, Dec. 5, 1973.

Radio, Television

40.   Walter Cronkite, "I Remember: Dag Hammar-
skjold," CBS telecast, "Twentieth Century," Oct. 28,
1962.

41.   Newscast, WKCT Radio, Bowling Green, Ky.,
Oct. 23, 1973.

Using material from another source

You may need to cite a work which you were not able to examine but which was
cited or quoted in another work. It is academically dishonest to indicate that you have
used a source if you have not done so. Cite in full the original source, then indicate the
source you used.

42.   Chicago Record, July 6, 1896, quoted in
Louis W. Koenig, Bryan (New York, 1971), 181.

SUBSEQUENT CITATIONS

The first citation must include all the publishing information that is required; this
same information is repeated in the bibliography where the reader can find a specific
item most readily. Subsequent footnote citations, however, do not have to be
complete. They should contain only enough information to guide the reader without
possibility of error to the first citation or to the entry in the bibliography.

The older style of footnoting subsequent citations made extensive use of the
author's last name and *op. cit. (opere citato*, in work cited) or *loc. cit. (loco citato*, in
the place cited). Such forms made ready identification difficult, and they were
especially confusing when one used several works by the same author. The modern
style of footnoting uses a short form which is designed to remind the reader of the full
citation which he has already seen. The short form should be meaningful in itself and
must be complete enough for ready recognition. If a long title is to be used frequently
(as in example 32 above), the author may provide a more drastic abbreviation, but he
must warn the reader what he is doing the first time the work is cited. And, once a
short form has been selected, it must be followed exactly thereafter.

The abbreviation *ibid. (ibidem*, in the same place) should be used if the citation is
the same as that in the last footnote with nothing intervening. *Ibid.* is capitalized only
if it is the first word in the note. It refers to the entire previous footnote except for
any differences which are indicated. *Ibid.* may also be used within a note when the
second (or later) reference repeats a portion of the first one. You may occasionally
find *ibid.* not underlined, but this is not yet generally accepted.

First citation to a book

43.   Richard N. Current, Secretary Stimson, A
Study in Statecraft (New Brunswick, New Jersey, 1954),
35.

Exactly the same as note 43 except for page number.

44.   Ibid., 40.

First citation to an article

45.   Thomas A. Bailey, "The Mythmakers of American History," <u>Journal</u> <u>of</u> <u>American</u> <u>History</u>, LV (June 1968), 8-10, 14.

Short form of book previously cited but with intervening material.

46.   Current, <u>Secretary</u> <u>Stimson</u>, 47.

Short form of article previously cited but with intervening material.

47.   Bailey, "The Mythmakers," 17.

First citation of two articles; ibid. refers only to the title of the journal.

48.   Richard S. Kirkendall, "The New Deal as Watershed: The Recent Literature," <u>Journal</u> <u>of</u> <u>American</u> <u>His-</u><u>tory</u>, LIV (March 1968), 839; William B. Hixson, Jr., "Moorfield Storey and the Struggle for Equality," <u>ibid.</u>, LX (Dec. 1968), 536.

First citation to printed correspondence; *ibid.* refers to the entire publishing information, including the volume number. Note that the full names of the men do not have to be repeated after the first time.

49.   Callender Irvine to John C. Calhoun, December 9, 1818, W. Edwin Hemphill, ed., <u>The</u> <u>Papers</u> <u>of</u> <u>John</u> <u>C.</u> <u>Calhoun</u> (9 vols. to date, Columbia, S.C., 1959-), III, 366-67; Calhoun to Irvine, December 18, 1818, <u>ibid.</u>, 403.

7
Bibliography

The purpose of the bibliography is to present at one place all of the sources used in the preparation of a paper or thesis. Thus a reader does not have to thumb through the footnotes to discover whether or not a particular source was used. If a work has been cited in a note, it should be included in the bibliography. Occasionally, a source may be included that was not cited but was of considerable use for background information; but as a general rule, do not include in the bibliography any source which can't be found in a footnote. (When you write a footnote, place a prominent check mark at the top of your bibliography card. Then, when you start writing the bibliography, pull out the marked cards and write your bibliography from them. When you start to cite a source in a footnote and the card is already marked, you know that you should use a short form.)

If a bibliography contains more than fifteen to twenty items, you will probably need to divide it. A very simple division consists of dividing the sources into "Primary" and "Secondary." More elaborate divisions will probably be determined by the types of sources which you have used. These will differ from topic to topic, but some of the most common are: manuscripts, government documents, interviews, newspapers, general histories, published correspondence, biographies, autobiographies and memoirs, general works, and articles. Arrange the sections in the order of importance to your research.

You may encounter a bibliography occasionally where the most logical organization seems to come from subdividing the topic itself. Such divisions are often made by topic or by chronology. If you use this pattern, each subdivision becomes a mini-bibliography which includes all sources relating to it.

Historians usually use one of three types of bibliography: the classified or traditional; the critical; and the annotated. Each has its own advantages and disadvantages, but modern scholarship is leaning more and more toward the critical essay form. (In many instances, however, you will use whatever form your instructor used in his graduate school.)

CLASSIFIED OR TRADITIONAL BIBLIOGRAPHY

This bibliography consists of a list (or lists, if subdivided) of the sources cited, arranged in alphabetical order by author. Its great merit is the ease with which one can check on a particular source. Its greatest weakness is the fact that all sources appear to have the same value. Two of the sources are listed together; each of them occupies the same amount of space. One was cited just once in a minor reference; the study could not have been written without the other; but they appear to be equally important.

In this type of bibliography the author's last name is listed first and the rest of the entry is indented five spaces so that the author's name stands out for ready reference. If an author has more than one title in the bibliography, list his name only once; in subsequent entries replace his name by an eight space line followed by a period. If a work has more than one author, place it according to the name of the first author listed. It is not customary to cross-file an entry under the name of each author. If an entry does not have an author, enter it under the heading which you feel will allow it to be found most easily. Single-space the items in a bibliography; double-space between them.

The following items have been listed by type of source to help you locate the needed example as quickly as possible; they have not been alphabetized as they would be in an actual bibliography.

BOOKS

Standard form

Storey, Moorfield. Charles Sumner. Boston, 1900.

Obscure place of publication

Baritz, Loren. The Servants of Power. Middleton, Conn., 1960.

Multi-editors, multi-volumed, published over several years

Emerson, Ralph Waldo. The Journal of Ralph Waldo Emerson. Edited by Edward Waldo Emerson and Waldo Emerson Forbes. 10 vols. Boston, 1909-14.

Later edition

Link, Arthur S. American Epoch: A History of the United States Since the 1890's. 2nd ed., rev. New York, 1963.

Sponsoring organization instead of author

Department of the Army. The United States in the World War, 1917-1919. 17 vols. Washington, 1948.

Date of first publication necessary

Mowry, George E. The California Progressives. Chicago, 1963; first published 1955.

Section of longer work

Davenport, Frederick M. "Did Hughes Snub Johnson? An Inside Story." The Politics of California. Edited by David Farrelly and Ivan Hinderacker. New York, 1951.

Part of multi-volumed work with general title

Craven, Avery O. The Growth of Southern Nationalism, 1848-1861. Vol. VI of A History of the South. Edited by Wendell Holmes Stephenson and E. Merton Coulter. 9 vols. to date. Baton Rouge, La., 1948-.

ARTICLES

Historical journal

Lasch, Christopher. "The Anti-Imperialists, The Philippines, and The Inequality of Man." Journal of Southern History, XXIV (Aug. 1958), 319-31.

Inclusive page numbers are given for articles.

Magazine, signed article

Bingham, Walter V. and James Rorty. "How the Army Sorts Its Manpower." Harper's Magazine, 185 (Sept. 1942), 432-40.

Magazine, unsigned, untitled

Newsweek, LXVIII (Aug. 22, 1966), 25.

Magazine, titled but unsigned

"Sex O'clock in America." Current Opinion, LV (Aug. 1913), 113-14.

PROCEEDINGS

Chinard, Gilbert. "The American Philosophical Society and the World of Science, 1768-1800." Proceedings of The American Philosophical Society, LXXXVII (1943).

NEWSPAPERS

Individual stories, unsigned, untitled

Gaelic American. New York. Dec. 21, 1918.

Republican. Springfield, Mass. Feb. 12, 1903.

Signed, titled article

Dix, Dorothy. "A Modern Diana." Boston American, April 7, 1910.

File of papers, not just specific items

Courier and New York Enquirer. June 1, 1856-Aug. 31, 1858.

MANUSCRIPTS

General collections

Bryan, William Jennings, Papers. Manuscript Division,
    Library of Congress.

House, Edward M., Papers. Yale University Library.

Specific items in collections

Dawes, Henry L. "Gen. Butler and Richard H. Dana."
    Henry L. Dawes Papers. Manuscript Division,
    Library of Congress.

Probate Court, St. Louis, Clerk's Office. Estate of
    John S. A. Sanford, No. 5328 (1858-1862).

Letter to author

Goff, John S., to author. April 19, 1969.

GOVERNMENT DOCUMENTS

Bureau of the Census, Department of Commerce. Eleventh
    Census of United States: 1890. Population. 25
    vols. Washington, 1894.

Congressional Record. 62 Cong., 2 Sess. (1912).
    Vols. IX-XXIII.

U.S. Statutes at Large. XXXVII, Parts I-III (Washing-
    ton, 1913).

War of the Rebellion: A Compilation of the Official
    Records of the Union and Confederate Armies.
    128 vols. Washington, 1880-1901. Series I,
    Vols. XXX-XXXVIII.

Example of collected official papers, correspondence, records, memoranda, telegrams,
etc., of federal government agencies:

United States National Archives, Washington, D.C.

Record Group 221, Records of the Rural Electrification
    Administration, General and Projects Correspondence
    of the Administration, 1936-1939.

Public Documents, general

Acts of Tennessee. 60 to 69 General Assembly, 1925-
    1935.

Federal Reporter Second Series Cases Argued and Deter-
    mined in the United States Circuit Court of Appeals,
    United States Court of Appeals for the District of

Columbia, United States Court of Customs and Patent
Appeals. St. Paul, 1935, 1937.

United States Reports: Cases Adjudged in the Supreme
Court. CCVC-CCCVIII (1934-1939), Washington,
1935-1940.

Report of the National Conservation Committee. 60 Cong.,
2 Sess., 1909.

Tennessee Valley Authority. A History of Navigation
on the Tennessee River System; An Interpretation
of the Economic Influence of This River System
on the Tennessee Valley. House Doc. 254, 75 Cong.,
1 Sess., Washington, 1937.

_____. Tennessee Valley Authority Handbook. TVA
Technical Library, Knoxville.

_____. Minutes, Board of Directors, 1933-1941,
Knoxville, 1933-1941.

_____. Press Releases, 1933-1941, Technical Library,
Knoxville, 1933-1941.

U.S. Congress. Senate. Committee on Agriculture and
Forestry. Amending the Tennessee Valley Authority
Act of 1933. 76 Cong., 1 Sess., 1939.

Annual Report of the Memphis Power and Light Company,
1933. Memphis, 1933.

Electric Power Board of Chattanooga. Annual Reports of
the Electric Power Board of Chattanooga for the
Fiscal Years Ended June 30, 1940-1961. Chattanooga,
1940-1961.

_____. Minutes, 1935-1961. Chattanooga, 1935-1961.

THESIS, DISSERTATION, UNPUBLISHED

Dalfiume, Richard M. "Desegregation of the United States
Armed Forces, 1939-1953." Doctoral dissertation,
University of Missouri, 1966.

INTERVIEWS

Smith, Gardner. Interview by James F. Howard, May 13,
1969. James F. Howard Collection. Kentucky
Library, Western Kentucky University.

Smith, Gardner. Interview by author, July 17, 1967.

CRITICAL BIBLIOGRAPHY

The critical bibliography is more difficult to write than either of the two other forms, and it is more difficult to scan in search of a particular item. But it has the great value of imparting to the reader the author's critical evaluation of the sources used. A well written critical essay on sources can be an invaluable guide to the literature on a particular topic. You should have some experience in writing such a bibliography although many of your instructors may assign one of the easier forms.

In making your critical judgments, remember that you are evaluating a work in regard to its value for your particular subject. Even an outstanding scholarly study may have little value for your specific subject. While it is hard to make a list of sources read like a novel, you should strive to make the essay as interesting as possible. Since it is an essay, you are expected to use complete sentences and well organized paragraphs. As in the case of the non-critical bibliography, some organization is essential; the form that it takes will depend upon your subject and your sources. If the general divisions are based on types of material, a logical organization is still required within each heading. Unless there is some good reason to do otherwise, you will start with your most impressive sources. You will sometimes get to the point where you can't think of anything to say about minor sources which were of little use. You can always dispose of them by some such sentence as: "These studies were of limited use:" and then listing them. And remember that one great advantage of the critical bibliography is that if you aren't certain of the proper form for an unused source you can just write a sentence or two about it. Do not use the possessive with the author's name in a bibliographical citation. In the following critical bibliography the correct form is Lowell H. Harrison, *John Breckinridge, Jeffersonian Republican*, not Lowell H. Harrison's, *John Breckinridge, Jeffersonian Republican.*

The bibliography below contains examples of the types of sources most commonly encountered. It is arranged primarily by types of sources to help in locating the examples you need.

Critical Essay on Sources

The most important source for this study was the collection of Breckinridge Manuscripts (Division of Manuscripts, Library of Congress). Containing over 100,000 items, the collection spans the years 1751-1948. Over 5,000 items relate to John Breckinridge. Also very useful, especially for the period 1801-1806, were the Jefferson Papers (Division of Manuscripts, Library of Congress) and the Madison Papers (Division of Manuscripts, Library of Congress). The John Brown

Papers in the Samuel M. Wilson Collection (University
of Kentucky) contain some Breckinridge letters, chiefly
on politics.

Portions of John Breckinridge's career may be
traced in government documents. Botetourt County
(Va.) Personal Property Tax Lists, 1783-1800 (Virginia
State Library, Richmond) and Fayette County (Ky.) Lists
of Taxable Property, 1793-1807 (Library of the Kentucky
State Historical Society, Frankfort) trace the accumu-
lation of his substantial estate. The Journals of the
House of Delegates of the Commonwealth of Virginia,
1781-1784 (Richmond, 1828) are the official record of
the Virginia lower house while Breckinridge was a mem-
ber. Especially important for his Kentucky years are
the House of Representatives Journals, 1794-1801. The
journals for 1794, 1796, 1797, and 1801 were used at
the Library of the Kentucky State Historical Society,
the first three in manuscript form. The Kentucky State
Library (Frankfort) has the 1795 and 1798 journals, and
a copy of the 1799 one is in the Massachusetts State
Library (Boston). No copy of the 1800 journal is
known to exist. The Debates and Proceedings in the
Congress of the United States (Washington, 1834-56),
42 vols., was the chief source of information about
Breckinridge's years in the Senate. The opinions
rendered by Breckinridge during his brief term as

Attorney General are in Benjamin F. Hall, ed., Official Opinions of the Attorneys General of the United States (Washington, 1852), I.

The Richmond Virginia Gazette supplied a great deal of general information about conditions in Virginia while Breckinridge was a resident of that state; Lester J. Cappon and Stella F. Duff, Virginia Gazette Index, 1736-1780 (Williamsburg, Va., 1950), 2 vols., was an invaluable guide. Once Breckinridge moved to Kentucky the Lexington Kentucky Gazette was indispensable for tracing his public career. The Lexington Public Library has an almost complete file which was read for the years 1793-1807. Especially useful for his years in Washington were the National Intelligencer and the Philadelphia Aurora, both Republican papers. They were frequently contradicted by the pro-Federalist Philadelphia Gazette of the United States.

Definitive editions of the correspondence of Jefferson and Madison are now being published, but neither has progressed far enough to be useful for this study. The best available editions are Albert E. Bergh and Andrew A. Libscomb, eds., The Writings of Jefferson (Washington, 1907), 20 vols., and Gaillard Hunt, ed., Writings of James Madison (New York, 1901-08), 9 vols., but both are incomplete and contain inaccuracies. A

few interesting items concerning national politics
were found in Elizabeth Donnan, ed., "Papers of James A.
Bayard, 1796-1815," in American Historical Association,
Annual Report, 1913 (Washington, 1915), II.

The only biography of John Breckenridge is Lowell
H. Harrison, John Breckinridge, Jeffersonian Republican
(Louisville, 1969). The author concludes that Breckinridge's outstanding public service came during his
first term in the Senate, 1801-1803, when he acted as
Jefferson's floor leader. Ethelbert D. Warfield, who
was related to the Breckinridges, published a biographical
sketch in The Kentucky Resolutions of 1798 (New York,
1887). Warfield overemphasized Breckenridge's role in
the drafting of the Kentucky Resolutions, but his study
is still sound in most respects. A brief account of
Breckinridge's life, based upon an account by one of
his sons, is in William H. Vaughn, Robert Jefferson
Breckinridge as an Educational Administrator, in
George Peabody College, Contributions to Education,
No. 208 (Nashville, 1937). A perceptive sketch of
Breckinridge's career is in James C. Klotter, "The
Breckinridges of Kentucky: Two Centuries of Leadership"
(doctoral dissertation, University of Kentucky, 1975).

John D. Barnhart, "Frontiersmen and Planters in
the Formation of Kentucky," Journal of Southern History,
VII (Feb. 1941), 19-36, stresses the role of the second

generation pioneer in the development of the state.   An excellent description of iron manufacturing is in J. Winston Coleman, Jr., "Old Kentucky Iron Furnaces," The Filson Club History Quarterly, 31 (July 1957), 227-42.

Of great use in ascertaining the relationship between Attorney General Breckinridge and President Jefferson was Rita W. Nealson, "Contributions of the Attorneys General to the Constitutional Development of the American Presidency" (doctoral dissertation, New York University, 1949).

ANNOTATED BIBLIOGRAPHY

The annotated bibliography appears to combine most of the advantages of the other two forms. It arranges the items in alphabetical order so that they are easily located, but it also includes the critical evaluation which is the great asset of the critical bibliography. Logic would seem to dictate general acceptance of this composite form.

In practice, it is used much less than either of the other types of bibliography. Like many middle-of-the-road decisions it displeases almost everyone, and examples are not readily located. But it does exist, and you should have some degree of familiarity with it.

The form of the annotated bibliography follows that of the classified bibliography. The critical comment follows immediately after the period which concludes the listing of a source; it is single-spaced and it follows the same pattern of reverse indentation as the bibliographical items. All sources do not have to carry critical comments. Routine sources which were little used should be left just as they are in the classified bibliography; add your evaluation (based on the sources used for your research project) only if the item had unusual value or was so unreliable as to merit a note of warning to the reader.

Consult the section on the classified bibliography for examples of the form. A few typical comments are shown below.

Clay, Cassius Marcellus. The Life of Cassius Marcellus Clay: Memoirs, Writings, and Speeches. Cincinnati, 1886. An interesting but very prejudiced autobiography. A projected second volume was never published.

The Writings of Cassius Marcellus Clay. Edited by Horace Greeley. New York, 1848. This collection consists mainly of speeches and editorials with few private letters.

Smiley, David L. Lion of White Hall. Madison, Wisc.,
     1962. A carefully researched, well-written volume
     which is the only complete biography of Clay.

Loria, Achille, Analisi della proprieta capitalista.
     Turin, Italy, 1889. The theories of this Italian
     economist were known to Turner, and they probably
     influenced his work.

Albion, Robert G. "The Communication Revolution."
     American Historical Review, XXXVII (July 1932),
     718-20. Stimulating essay.

Billington, Ray A. "Frederick Jackson Turner--
     Universal Historian." In Frontier and Section:
     Selected Essays of Frederick Jackson Turner.
     Englewood Cliffs, New Jersey, 1961. Extremely
     helpful introduction to these important essays.

Extra Census Bulletin No. 12, April 20, 1891. Early
     statement of the "end of the frontier."

Wilson, Woodrow. "The Making of the Nation." Atlantic
     Monthly, LXXX (July 1897), 1-14. Presents views
     on the development of the nation.

Wright, Benjamin F. "Review of Frederick J. Turner's
     Significance of Sections in American History."
     New England Quarterly, VI (Sept. 1933), 630-34.

LIBRARY EXERCISE

This exercise is designed to help you find sources in your library. There are two blank spaces following each question; use the first (A) to list the information found, and the second (B) to indicate the source of that information.

1. The names of all the Spanish missions still in existence in San Antonio, Texas.

    A.

    B.

2. A newspaper account of the Centennial Exposition in Philadelphia, Pennsylvania, in 1876.

    A.

    B.

3. Listing of five reviews of Ray Allen Billington, *Westward Expansion.*

    A.

    B.

4. An eyewitness account of the burning of the dirigible *Zepplin.*

    A.

    B.

5. The location of the presidential papers of Harry S Truman.

    A.

    B.

6. A brief biography of Benjamin Disraeli.

    A.

    B.

7. Location of the personal papers of Joseph Holt.

    A.

    B.

8. Names of members of the House of Representatives Committee on Agriculture, 73rd Congress, 1st Session.

    A.

    B.

9. Complete bibliographical information for a book titled *Cabinet Politician.*

    A.

    B.

10. Complete title of a United States Senate hearing on the Tennessee Valley Authority bill.

    A.

    B.

11. A magazine article on Buffalo Bill.

    A.

    B.

12. The declaration of the existence of a state of war between the United States and Japan.

    A.

    B.

13. The title of two (2) newspapers published in Boston, Massachusetts in 1863.

    A.

    B.

14. The title (or "style") of a case adjudged by the United States Supreme Court in 1874; of a case adjudged in 1937.

    A.

    B.

15. The number and a description of the patent awarded to Abraham Lincoln for an improvement for steamboats.

    A.

    B.

PROBLEMS IN HISTORICAL CRITICISM

1. Roy N. Lokken, "Has the Mystery of 'A Public Man' Been Solved?," *Mississippi Valley Historical Review*, XL (Dec. 1953), 419-40.

   Frank M. Anderson, "Has the Mystery of 'A Public Man' Been Solved? — A Rejoinder," *Mississippi Valley Historical Review*, XLII (June 1955), 101-107.

   Roy N. Lokken, "A Reply to 'A Rejoinder'," *Mississippi Valley Historical Review*, XLII (June 1955), 107-109.

2. Joseph C. Rayback, "Who Wrote the Allison Letters: A Study in Historical Detection," *Mississippi Valley Historical Review*, XXXVI (June 1949), 51-72.

3. "The Horn Papers," *Mississippi Valley Historical Review*, XXXIV (Dec. 1947), 528-30. For a more complete analysis, see Arthur Pierce Middleton and Douglass Adair, "The Mystery of the Horn Papers," *William and Mary Quarterly*, 3rd series, IV (Oct. 1947), 409-45.

4. Milo M. Quaife, "A Critical Evaluation of the Sources for Western History," *Mississippi Valley Historical Review*, I (Sept. 1914), 167-84.

5. Max Farrand, ed., *The Records of the Federal Convention* of 1787(4 vols., New Haven, 1911-37), III, Appendix D, 596-609.

6. Howard K. Beale, "Is the Printed Diary of Gideon Welles Reliable?," *American Historical Review*, XXX (April 1925), 547-52.

7. Thomas A. Bailey, "The Russian Fleet Myth Re-examined," *Mississippi Valley Historical Review*, XXXVIII (June 1951), 81-90.

8. Quentin Reynolds, "The Man Who Wouldn't Talk," *Reader's Digest*, 63 (Nov. 1953), 157-80. Then see: 64 (Jan. 1954), 106-108.

9. Hayes Baker-Crothers and Ruth Allison Hudnut, "A Private Soldier's Account of Washington's First Battles in the West: A Study in Historical Criticism," *Journal of Southern History*, VIII (Feb. 1942), 23-62.

10. Robert Allen Skotheim, "A Note on Historical Method: David Donald's 'Toward a Reconsideration of Abolitionists'," *Journal of Southern History*, XXV (Aug. 1959), 356-65.

11. Horace Montgomery, "The Two Howell Cobbs: A Case of Mistaken Identity," *Journal of Southern History*, XXVIII (Aug. 1962), 348-55.

12. Robert D. Clark, "Bishop Matthew Simpson and the Emancipation Proclamation," *Mississippi Valley Historical Review*, XXXV (Sept. 1948), 263-71.

13. Ludwell H. Johnson, "Lincoln and Equal Rights: The Authenticity of the Wadsworth Letter," *Journal of Southern History*, XXXII (Feb. 1966), 83-87.

14. James L. Anderson and W. Edwin Hemphill, "The 1843 Biography of John C. Calhoun: Was R. M. T. Hunter Its Author?," *Journal of Southern History*, XXXVIII (Aug. 1972), 469-74.

15. June I. Gow, "The Johnston and Brent Diaries: A Problem of Authorship," *Civil War History*, 14 (March 1968), 46-50.

16. Helen Rand Parish and Harold E. Weidman, "The Correct Birthdate of Barolomé de las Casas," *Hispanic American Historical Review*, LVI (Aug. 1976), 385-403.

17. Ernest J. Burrus, "Two Fictitious Accounts of Ortega's 'Third Voyage' to California," *Hispanic American Historical Review*, LII (May 1972), 272-83.

18. Benjamin Keen, "The Black Legend Revisited: Assumptions and Realities," *Hispanic American Historical Review*, XLIX (Nov. 1969), 703-19.

Lewis Hanke, "A Modest Proposal for a Moratorium on Grand Generalizations: Some Thoughts on the Black Legend," *Hispanic American Historical Review*, LI (Feb. 1971), 112-27.

Benjamin Keen, "The White Legend Revisited: A Reply to Professor Hanke's 'Modest Proposal'," *Hispanic American Historical Review*, LI (May 1971), 336-55.

After reading one of these examples of historical criticism, complete the exercise on page 61.

A PROBLEM IN HISTORICAL CRITICISM

Your Name: Class:

Article Read:

The problem:

How resolved:

Type of historical criticism used:

FOOTNOTE EXERCISE

Put these footnotes in the proper form as they would appear in a paper.

1. Basil W. Duke published *A History of Morgan's Cavalry* in Cincinnati, 1867; you used a reprint edition that was published in Bloomington, Indiana in 1960 by the Indiana University Press. Your reference is to page 75.

2. The University Press of Kentucky, Lexington, in 1975 published Edison H. Thomas' book, *John Hunt Morgan and His Raiders.* On page 79 he quotes from page 212 of John J. McAfee, *Kentucky Politicians,* that was published in 1886 in Louisville, Kentucky, by the *Courier-Journal* Job Printing Co. You were not able to find a copy of McAfee's book.

3. C. A. Evans edited a 12 volume set called *Confederate Military History* that was published in Atlanta, Georgia, in 1899 by the Confederate Publishing Company. You have used the volume called *Kentucky* that was written by J. Stoddard Johnston; it is volume IX. Your reference is to page 191.

4. An article, "Basil Wilson Duke, 1838-1916," appeared in *The Filson Club History Quarterly* for April, 1940. The article was on pages 59-64. Your reference is to a footnote on page 61. The issue is No. 2 in Volume 14. James W. Henning was the author.

5. *John Hunt Morgan and His Raiders,* written by Edison H. Thomas, was published in Lexington by the University Press of Kentucky in 1975. The material you are using is on page 37.

6. The University Press of Kentucky, Lexington, published Edison H. Thomas' book, *John Hunt Morgan and His Raiders* in 1975. You want to cite something from page 37 of this book.

7. John H. Morgan wrote a letter to his wife on January 2, 1863. You found this letter in the Duke-Morgan Family Papers in the Southern Historical Collection at the University of North Carolina.

8. On June 6, 1977 you interviewed Jane M. Smith, a granddaughter of D. Howard Smith, at her home in Philadelphia.

Index